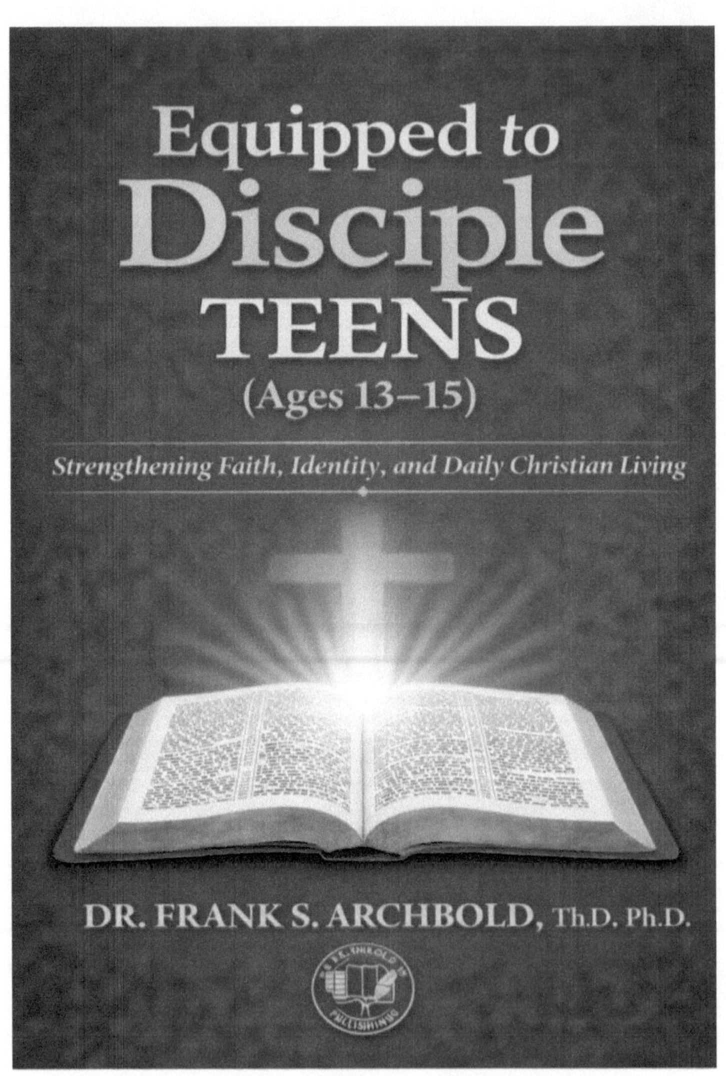

Equipped to
Disciple
TEENS
(Ages 13–15)

Strengthening Faith, Identity, and Daily Christian Living

DR. FRANK S. ARCHBOLD, Th.D. Ph.D.

PUBLISHING INFORMATION

Published by: **F. S. Archbold Publishing LLC** Edition: **Youth Edition** Language:
English Year of Publication: **2026**

DISCLAIMER

This work is not intended to replace pastoral teaching, personal counseling, or the spiritual oversight of a local church. Readers are encouraged to apply the biblical principles presented herein under the guidance of the Holy Spirit and in fellowship with spiritually mature leaders.

Printed in the United States of America

ISBN: 978-1-971265-16-2

TABLE OF CONTENTS

DEDICATION

This book is dedicated first and foremost to the **Lord Jesus Christ**, the Author and Finisher of our faith, whose love, grace, and truth transform lives and call each generation to follow Him faithfully.

I dedicate this Teen Edition to the **young men and women** who are seeking truth, identity, and purpose in a world filled with confusion, pressure, and competing voices. May these pages help you know Christ personally, walk confidently in your faith, and live courageously for Him in every season of life.

With deep gratitude, I dedicate this work to my wife, **Suzzette Archbold**, my faithful companion in life and ministry, whose prayers, support, and unwavering devotion continue to strengthen both my calling and our family. I also dedicate this book to our children—**Fransheska, Abigail, Frank Jr., and Jonathan**—and to our grandchildren, whose lives remind me daily of the importance of intentional discipleship across generations.

This book is further dedicated to **parents, pastors, youth leaders, teachers, and mentors** who labor faithfully to guide the next generation in the Word of God. Your investment, prayers, and example shape lives far beyond what is seen.

May this book serve as a tool to strengthen faith, form godly character, and raise a generation of disciples who love God, honor His Word, and boldly fulfill the Great Commission—for the glory of God and the advancement of His Kingdom.

ABOUT THE AUTHOR

Dr. Frank S. Archbold, Th.D., Ph.D., is a pastor, bishop, theologian, Christian counselor, and author with more than four decades of ministry experience dedicated to discipleship, spiritual formation, and leadership development within the Christian Church.

He was born on April 23, 1961, in the province of Bocas del Toro, Republic of Panama. At the age of twelve, he accepted Jesus Christ as his personal Savior at Jordan Baptist Church under the pastoral leadership of his father—an experience that marked the beginning of a lifelong calling to ministry and service to the Gospel.

In 1983, Dr. Archbold emigrated to the United States in obedience to the Great Commission, devoting himself to preaching, teaching, and forming disciples across generations. He was ordained as an evangelist and later as a minister of the Word, serving in various capacities that include pastoral leadership, worship ministry, biblical teaching, and Christian counseling. In 1995, he was ordained to the office of Bishop.

Dr. Archbold is the founder and overseer of **Covenant Keepers Ministries International**, a work committed to building strong believers, healthy churches, and Christ-centered communities. His ministry has extended internationally, with significant service in both the United States and the Republic of Panama. He has also served in leadership roles related to pastoral councils, ecumenical committees, chaplaincy programs, and Christian rehabilitation initiatives.

With a deep burden for the next generation, Dr. Archbold has invested heavily in **youth discipleship**, Christian education, and family-centered faith formation. He believes that biblical truth, when taught clearly and lived authentically, has the power to shape identity, strengthen character, and guide young people through the challenges of today's world.

He is the author of the *Equipped to Disciple* series, designed to provide structured, Scripture-centered discipleship for children, teens, youth, and adults. His teaching style combines solid biblical doctrine, pastoral sensitivity, and practical application for daily Christian living.

Dr. Archbold has been married for more than forty years to his wife, **Suzzette Archbold**, with whom he shares both family life and ministry calling. They are the parents of four children and grandparents to several grandchildren. He firmly believes that the family is a foundational pillar of Christian faith and an essential context for effective discipleship.

Through his writing and ministry, Dr. Frank S. Archbold remains committed to forming disciples who know Christ, live according to His Word, and faithfully fulfill God's purpose in their generation.

INTRODUCTION
Equipped to Disciple Teens
Strengthening Faith, Identity, and Daily Christian Living

The Christian life begins with a personal encounter with Jesus Christ—but it does not end there. Salvation is the starting point of a journey that leads to growth, transformation, and purpose. The Bible calls this journey **discipleship**.

Jesus did not simply invite people to believe in Him; He called them to **follow Him**, learn from Him, and live according to His teachings. In a world filled with confusion, pressure, and many competing voices, discipleship helps young believers know who they are, what they believe, and how to live faithfully every day.

This book was written especially for **teenagers**—young men and women who are navigating critical years of identity formation, decision-making, and spiritual growth.

During this stage of life, questions naturally arise:

- *¿Who am I?*
- *¿Why do I exist?*
- *¿What does it mean to follow Jesus today?*
- *¿How do I live my faith at school, at home, and with my friends?*

The purpose of *Equipped to Disciple Teens* is to provide clear, biblical answers to those questions and to guide you step by step in building a strong foundation of faith.

"Go ye therefore, and teach all nations... teaching them to observe all things whatsoever I have commanded you." *(Matthew 28:19–20)*

A MANUAL FOR REAL LIFE

This book is not meant to be read quickly and forgotten. It is designed as a **discipleship manual**—a tool that can be used:
- Individually, for personal growth
- In youth groups or small groups
- In Christian schools or discipleship classes
- With parents, mentors, or youth leaders

Each chapter addresses an essential area of the Christian life, moving from **identity in Christ**, to **spiritual disciplines**, to **Christian character**, and finally to **living out your faith with purpose and mission**.

Throughout the book you will find:
- Real-life teen scenarios
- Key Bible verses from the Word of God
- Practical applications for everyday life
- Questions for reflection and group discussion
- Guided prayers and memory verses

These elements are designed to help you not only **understand** the truth, but also **live it**.

DISCIPLESHIP IS A JOURNEY

Discipleship is not about perfection—it is about direction. It is a daily decision to grow, to learn, and to follow Jesus more closely. Every believer grows at a different pace, and God is patient and faithful as we walk with Him.

This book recognizes that:
- You may be new to faith, or already growing
- You may have questions, doubts, or struggles
- You may be learning how to apply biblical truth in real situations

God is not discouraged by honest questions. He invites you to seek Him, to learn His Word, and to allow the Holy Spirit to guide you into truth.

A CALL TO GROW AND COMMIT

Discipleship is not just about receiving information—it is about transformation. As you work through these chapters, you are invited to:

- Grow deeper in your relationship with God
- Develop Christlike character
- Learn to pray, worship, and serve
- Discover your gifts and purpose
- Share your faith with love and confidence

Jesus calls every believer to move from simply believing to actively **living and discipling others**.

OPENING PRAYER

Lord God,

Open my heart and my understanding to receive Your Word. Help me grow in faith, wisdom, and obedience. Guide my steps as I learn to follow Jesus and live according to Your will. Use my life for Your glory and help me become a true disciple of Christ. In Jesus' name. Amen.

May the Holy Spirit use this book to strengthen your faith, shape your identity, and guide you into a life that honors God and blesses others.

CHAPTER 1
WHY WAS I CREATED?
Purpose, Identity, and Value in God

Key Verse

"Thou art worthy, O Lord, to receive glory and honour and power: for thou hast created all things, and for thy pleasure they are and were created." — Revelation 4:11

Opening Thought

One of the biggest questions every teenager asks—sometimes out loud, sometimes quietly—is this:

"¿Why am I here?"

If you don't know the answer to that question, it's easy to feel lost, pressured, or confused. But the Bible gives a clear answer and it changes everything.

Real Life Scenario — *"¿Do I Even Matter?"*

Daniel is 14 years old.

At school, he feels average. He's not the best athlete, not the smartest student, and not the most popular. When he scrolls through social media, it feels like everyone else has something he doesn't—confidence, talent, friends, or a perfect life. One night, after another long day of comparison, Daniel puts his phone down and stares at the ceiling. A thought comes into his mind: *"¿Why am I even here? Does my life really matter?"*

He believes in God. He goes to church. But deep inside, he feels invisible. Daniel's struggle is not unique. Many teens feel this way—even those who love God. The problem isn't that God didn't create them with purpose. The problem is that they haven't yet discovered **why** they were created.

This chapter exists to answer that question.

Big Truth

You were created on purpose, by God, and for God. Your life is **not an accident**. You are **not random**. You are **not a mistake**.

Biblical Foundation — Created by God

"In the beginning God created the heaven and the earth." — Genesis 1:1

Everything starts with God. Before schools, careers, families, or social media—**God existed**. And He created all things with intention.

"And God said; Let us make man in our image, after our likeness." — Genesis 1:26

This means:
- You were created **by God**
- You were created **like God** (with value, dignity, and purpose)
- You were created **for God**

Created for God's Glory

Revelation 4:11 teaches that everything was created for God's pleasure. This does not mean God is selfish. It means He created us to live in relationship with Him and to reflect who He is. A phone is created to communicate. A car is created to transport. A watch is created to tell time. If something does not fulfill its purpose, it does not function well.

In the same way, **a human life only makes sense when it lives for God**.

Identity vs. Labels

The world constantly tries to label teens:
- Smart or not
- Popular or ignored
- Athletic or "not good enough"
- Attractive or insecure

But God gives a different identity.

"For we are his workmanship, created in Christ Jesus unto good works." — Ephesians 2:10

You are **God's workmanship**. That means:
- Designed carefully
- Created intentionally
- Valuable by nature

Your worth does not come from likes, grades, or opinions. Your worth comes from **who created you**.

Why Purpose Matters

When a teen doesn't know their purpose:
- They follow the crowd
- They compare constantly
- They make decisions based on pressure
- They look for acceptance in the wrong places

When a teen knows their purpose:
- They gain confidence
- They make wiser choices
- They resist peer pressure
- They grow spiritually stronger

Purpose brings direction.
Direction brings stability.

Faith Meets Real Life

At School

Knowing you were created by God helps you:
- Stand firm when others mock your faith
- Value learning as a gift from God
- Treat others with respect

With Friends

You don't need to change who you are to be accepted. God created you with intention.

Online

Social media shows highlights—not reality. Your value is not measured by comparison.

In Decisions

When you know why you exist, you ask better questions:
- *¿Does this honor God?*
- *¿Does this align with my purpose?*

God's Will and Your Life

The word **will** in Revelation 4:11 means:
- Purpose
- Desire
- Intention

This means God **wanted** you to exist.

"The steps of a good man are ordered by the LORD." — Psalm 37:23

God's will is not about controlling you—it's about guiding you.

Pastoral Warning

One of the enemy's greatest strategies is distraction—keeping teens busy but without purpose.

You can attend church, activities, and events, yet still feel empty if you don't know **why you live for God**.

Discipleship exists to answer that "why."

Discussion Questions

1. ¿Why do many teens struggle with identity today?
2. ¿How does social media affect how teens see themselves?
3. ¿What does it mean that you were created for God's pleasure?
4. ¿How would your choices change if you truly believed your life has purpose?
5. ¿What labels have you believed that God never gave you?

Action Step (This Week)

Daily Purpose Reminder
- Every morning this week, say out loud: *"I was created by God, for God, and my life has purpose."*
- Write one way you can honor God each day (attitude, decision, kindness).

Prayer

Lord God,

Thank You for creating me with purpose. Forgive me for believing lies about my value. Help me stop comparing myself to others and teach me to see myself the way You see me. I want to live for You and honor You with my life. In Jesus' name. Amen.

Memory Verse

"I will praise thee; for I am fearfully and wonderfully made." — Psalm 139:14

PERSONAL NOTES & ASSIGNMENT REFLECTION
Chapter 1
Personal Notes

Use this space to write your thoughts, questions, key ideas, Scripture verses, insights, or practical applications from this chapter. Reflect on how the truths you are learning apply to your daily life, decisions, and relationships.

"Thy word is a lamp unto my feet, and a light unto my path."
(Psalm 119:105)

Assignment Reflection (if applicable)

____

____

____

____

____

____

____

____

____

____

____

____

____

____

____

____

____

____

____

____

____

____

____

____

____

____

Date: _______________________________

Signature / Initials: _______________________________

CHAPTER 2

¿HOW CAN I BE SAVED?
Grace, Faith, and a New Life in Christ

Key Verse
"Believe on the Lord Jesus Christ, and thou shalt be saved." —
Acts 16:31

Opening Thought

One of the most important questions a person can ever ask is
not about school, success, or the future—but this:

"¿Am I right with God?"

Many teens attend church, know Bible stories, and believe God
exists, yet still feel unsure about salvation. This chapter explains
clearly, simply, and biblically how a person can be saved and live
with confidence and peace.

Real Life Scenario — *"¿Am I Really Saved?"*

Sofia is 15 years old. She grew up in church and knows the right
answers in Bible class. But lately, she feels confused. She still
struggles with temptation, gets angry, and sometimes says things
she regrets.

One night she asks herself: *"¿If I were really saved, wouldn't I be
better than this?"*

She wonders if salvation is something she can lose every time
she fails—or if she was ever saved at all. Sofia's struggle is
common among teens who love God but don't yet understand
what salvation truly means.

This chapter is written for teens like Sofia.

Big Truth

Salvation is not earned by being perfect—it is received by trusting Jesus.

¿What Is Salvation?

The word **salvation** means *deliverance*. In the Bible, salvation is God rescuing us from the power of sin and restoring us to a relationship with Him.

"For the wages of sin is death; but the gift of God is eternal life through Jesus Christ our Lord." — Romans 6:23

Sin separates people from God—not only big, obvious sins, but all disobedience. That is why everyone needs salvation.

"For all have sinned, and come short of the glory of God." — Romans 3:23

Salvation is not about becoming religious. It is about being made new.

¿Why Do We Need to Be Saved?

1. Sin Separates Us from God: Sin breaks fellowship with God and brings spiritual death.
2. We Cannot Save Ourselves: Good behavior, church attendance, and kindness cannot erase sin. "Not by works of righteousness which we have done, but according to his mercy he saved us." — Titus 3:5
3. God Loves Us Too Much to Leave Us Lost: *"For God so loved the world that he gave his one and only Son*, that whoever believes in him shall not perish but have eternal life" - John 3:16

¿How did God provide salvation?

God's answer to sin was **Jesus Christ.**

"But God commendeth his love toward us, in that, while we were yet sinners, Christ died for us." — Romans 5:8

Jesus:
- Lived a sinless life
- Died on the cross for our sins
- Rose again on the third day

"Who was delivered for our offences, and was raised again for our justification." — Romans 4:25

¿How Can I Be Saved?

The Bible gives a clear and simple answer.

1. Admit Your Need: "For all have sinned, and come short of the glory of God"— Romans 3:23 - Salvation begins with honesty.
2. Believe in Jesus Christ: "That if thou shalt confess with thy mouth the Lord Jesus, and shalt believe in thine heart, that God hath raised him from the dead, thou shalt be saved" — Romans 10:9–10 - Belief is not just knowledge—it is trust.
3. Receive Salvation by Faith: "For by grace are ye saved through faith; and that not of yourselves: it is the gift of God. Not of works, lest any man should boast" — Ephesians 2:8–9

What Salvation Is—and What It Is Not

Salvation IS:
- A gift of grace
- A new beginning
- A restored relationship with God

Salvation is NOT:
- A reward for good behavior
- Perfection without struggle
- A license to sin

"If any man be in Christ, he is a new creature." — 2 Corinthians 5:17

Can I Know That I Am Saved?

Yes. God wants believers to have assurance.

"These things have I written unto you that believe… that ye may know that ye have eternal life." — 1 John 5:13

Salvation confidence comes from trusting God's Word—not feelings.

Faith Meets Real Life

- **When You Fail:** Failure does not cancel salvation. Confession restores fellowship. "If we confess our sins, he is faithful and just to forgive us." — 1 John 1:9}
- **When You Doubt:** Return to God's promises, not your emotions.
- **When You Grow:** Salvation begins instantly, but growth takes time.

A New Life Begins

Salvation produces change—not overnight perfection, but new direction.

"My sheep hear my voice, and I know them, and they follow me." — John 10:27

A saved teen:

- Desires God
- Feels conviction when sinning
- Wants to grow spiritually

Discussion Questions
1. ¿What is salvation according to the Bible?
2. ¿Why can't good works save us?
3. ¿What does it mean to trust Jesus personally?
4. ¿Why do teens struggle with assurance of salvation?
5. ¿How does salvation change daily life?

Action Step (This Week)
- Read Romans chapter 10.
- Write a short prayer thanking God for His grace.
- If unsure about salvation, talk with a pastor or leader.

Prayer

Lord God, I acknowledge that I need You. I believe that Jesus Christ died for my sins and rose again. I receive Your grace and forgiveness by faith. Help me grow in my new life and trust Your promises. In Jesus' name. Amen.

Memory Verse

"For by grace are ye saved through faith; and that not of yourselves: it is the gift of God." — Ephesians 2:8

PERSONAL NOTES & ASSIGNMENT REFLECTION
Chapter 2
Personal Notes

Use this space to write your thoughts, questions, key ideas, Scripture verses, insights, or practical applications from this chapter. Reflect on how the truths you are learning apply to your daily life, decisions, and relationships.

"Thy word is a lamp unto my feet, and a light unto my path." *(Psalm 119:105)*

Assignment Reflection (if applicable)

____ 27
____
____
____
____
____
____
____
____
____
____
____
____
____
____
____
____
____
____
____
____
____
____
____
____

Date: _______________________________

Signature / Initials: _______________________________

CHAPTER 3
WATER BAPTISM
Obedience, Identity, and a Public Faith

Key Verse

"Therefore we are buried with him by baptism into death: that like as Christ was raised up from the dead by the glory of the Father, even so we also should walk in newness of life." — Romans 6:4

Opening Thought

After a person believes in Jesus Christ and receives salvation, a natural question follows:

"¿What should I do next?"

The Bible gives a clear answer. One of the first steps of obedience in the Christian life is **water baptism**. Baptism does not save us, but it powerfully declares that we belong to Jesus.

Real Life Scenario — *"¿What Will People Think?"*

Luis is 13 years old. He accepted Jesus as his Savior a few months ago. His heart has changed, and he wants to follow God seriously. When his youth leader announces an upcoming baptism service, Luis feels excited—but also nervous.
He begins to think:

"What if my friends laugh?"
"What if my family doesn't understand?"
"What if I'm not ready?"

Luis wants to obey Jesus, but fear of people's opinions holds him back. Many teens face this same struggle. This chapter will help answer those fears with biblical truth.

Big Truth
Baptism is a public declaration that I belong to Jesus.

¿What Is Water Baptism?

The word *baptism* comes from the Greek word **baptō**, which means *to immerse.* Biblical baptism is performed by fully immersing a person in water.

Baptism represents three powerful truths:

- **Death** to the old life of sin
- **Burial** with Christ
- **Resurrection** to a new life in Him

"Buried with him in baptism, wherein also ye are risen with him through the faith of the operation of God." — Colossians 2:12

¿Why should we be baptized?

1. Because Jesus Commanded It: "Go ye therefore, and teach all nations, baptizing them…" — Matthew 28:19 - Baptism is not a church tradition—it is a command from Jesus Himself.
2. Because Jesus Was Baptized: "Then cometh Jesus from Galilee to Jordan unto John, to be baptized of him." — Matthew 3:13 - If Jesus, who never sinned, chose to be baptized, ¿how much more should we follow His example?
3. Because Baptism Identifies Us With Christ: Baptism declares that our old life is over and a new life has begun.

What Baptism Is—and What It Is Not

Baptism IS:
- An act of obedience
- A public testimony of faith
- A symbol of inner transformation

Baptism is NOT:
- A requirement for salvation
- A magical act
- A guarantee of perfection

"For by grace are ye saved through faith…" — Ephesians 2:8

¿When Should a Person Be Baptized?

The Bible shows a clear pattern: baptism follows belief.

"Then they that gladly received his word were baptized." — Acts 2:41

A person should be baptized when they:
- Have believed in Jesus Christ
- Understand the meaning of baptism
- Desire to obey the Lord

Age is not the main requirement—**faith is**.

¿Who Can Baptize?

Jesus gave authority to His disciples and the Church to baptize believers.

"Go ye therefore…" — Matthew 28:19

Today, baptism is normally administered by pastors or church leaders under the authority of the local church.

¿How is Baptism Performed?

Biblical baptism is done:
- By immersion in water
- In the name of the Father, Son, and Holy Ghost

"Baptizing them in the name of the Father, and of the Son, and of the Holy Ghost." — Matthew 28:19

Baptism may take place in rivers, pools, lakes, or baptismal tanks.

"See, here is water; what doth hinder me to be baptized?" — Acts 8:36

Faith Meets Real Life

- **Fear of People:** "For do I now persuade men, or God?" - Galatians 1:10 - Baptism is about pleasing God, not impressing people.
- **Fear of Failure:** Baptism does not mean you will never struggle again—it means you are committed to following Jesus.
- **Fear of Not Being Ready:** Obedience often comes before confidence. Faith grows as we obey.

¿What Happens After Baptism?

Baptism marks a new beginning.

After baptism, a believer should:

- Continue learning God's Word
- Pray daily
- Attend church regularly
- Walk in obedience

"Teaching them to observe all things whatsoever I have commanded you." — Matthew 28:20

Discussion Questions

1. ¿What does water baptism represent?
2. ¿Why did Jesus command baptism?
3. ¿What fears can keep teens from being baptized?
4. ¿Why is obedience important in the Christian life?
5. ¿How does baptism strengthen faith?

Action Step (This Week)

- Talk with a pastor, youth leader, or parent about baptism.
- Read Romans chapter 6.
- Pray and ask God to give you courage to obey.

Prayer

Lord Jesus, thank You for saving me and calling me to follow You. Give me courage to obey You openly and faithfully. Help me walk in newness of life and live unashamed of my faith. In Your name I pray. Amen.

Memory Verse

"He that believeth and is baptized shall be saved." — Mark 16:16

Chapter 3
Personal Notes

Use this space to write your thoughts, questions, key ideas, Scripture verses, insights, or practical applications from this chapter. Reflect on how the truths you are learning apply to your daily life, decisions, and relationships.

"Thy word is a lamp unto my feet, and a light unto my path."
(Psalm 119:105)

____
____
____
____
____
____
____
____
____
____
____
____
____
____
____
____
____
____
____
____
____
____
____

Assignment Reflection (if applicable)

____
____
____
____
____
____
____
____
____
____
____
____
____
____
____
____
____
____
____
____
____
____
____
____
____
____
____
____
____

Date: _______________________________

Signature / Initials: _______________________________

CHAPTER 4
THE BIBLE
God's Word, Truth, and Direction for Daily Life

Key Verse

"Thy word is a lamp unto my feet, and a light unto my path." —
Psalm 119:105

Opening Thought

Every teen is searching for direction. Questions about identity,
decisions, relationships, and the future come early in life. The
Bible teaches that God did not leave us without guidance. He
gave us His Word so that we could know Him, understand truth,
and walk the right path.

The Bible is not an old or irrelevant book. It is God's living voice
for today.

Real Life Scenario — *"I Don't Get the Bible"*

Emily is 14 years old. She owns a Bible and brings it to church,
but when she tries to read it at home, she feels confused. Some
verses make sense, others feel distant, and sometimes she gets
bored and puts it down.

She wonders: *"¿If the Bible is so important, why is it so hard to
understand?"*

Emily's experience is common. Many teens love God but struggle
to connect with Scripture. This chapter will help remove fear,
confusion, and frustration from reading the Bible.

Big Truth
The Bible is God's Word, and it speaks clearly to those who seek Him.

¿What is the Bible?

The Bible is the inspired Word of God, written by human authors under the guidance of the Holy Spirit.

"All scripture is given by inspiration of God." — 2 Timothy 3:16

Although written over many years by different authors, the Bible has one message: God's plan to redeem humanity through Jesus Christ.

"For the prophecy came not in old time by the will of man: but holy men of God spoke as they were moved by the Holy Ghost." — 2 Peter 1:21

¿Why Can We Trust the Bible?

1. It Comes From God: God does not lie or make mistakes. - "God is not a man, that he should lie." — Numbers 23:19
2. Jesus Trusted the Scriptures: "It is written…" — Matthew 4:4 Jesus used Scripture as truth and authority.
3. The Bible Changes Lives: "For the word of God is quick, and powerful." — Hebrews 4:12

¿How Is the Bible Organized?

The Bible contains **66 books**, divided into two main sections:

- **The Old Testament (39 books):** Reveals God's creation, covenant, law, and promises.

- **The New Testament (27 books):** Reveals Jesus Christ, salvation, and the Church.

The Old Testament prepares the way for Christ; the New Testament fulfills it.

"Think not that I am come to destroy the law… but to fulfill." — Matthew 5:17

¿Why should Teens read the Bible?

1. To Know God Personally: "Draw nigh to God, and he will draw nigh to you." — James 4:8
2. To Grow spiritually: "As newborn babes, desire the sincere milk of the word." — 1 Peter 2:2
3. To Make Wise Decisions: "Thy word have I hid in mine heart, that I might not sin against thee." — Psalm 119:11
4. To Stand against Pressure: "And take… the sword of the Spirit, which is the word of God." — Ephesians 6:17

¿How to Read the Bible Effectively?

1. Pray before you read: "Open thou mine eyes, that I may behold wondrous things out of thy law." — Psalm 119:18
2. Read daily, not Randomly: Consistency matters more than length.
3. Start with understandable books: Recommended starting points:
   * Gospel of John
   * Proverbs
   * Psalms
   * Romans
4. Apply What You Read: "Be ye doers of the word, and not hearers only." — James 1:22

Faith Meets Real Life

- **At School:** God's Word helps you choose honesty, integrity, and kindness.
- **With Friends:** Scripture teaches discernment and love.
- **Online:** The Bible helps you recognize truth from lies.
- **In Temptation:** God's Word strengthens self-control.

The Bible and the Local Church

God designed Scripture to be taught, explained, and lived within the church.

"And they continued steadfastly in the apostles' doctrine." — Acts 2:42

The church helps believers:
- Understand Scripture
- Apply truth
- Grow together

Pastoral Warning

Ignoring God's Word weakens faith. Spiritual confusion grows when Scripture is neglected.

"My people are destroyed for lack of knowledge." — Hosea 4:6

Discussion Questions

1. ¿Why do some teens struggle to read the Bible?
2. ¿How does God speak through Scripture?
3. ¿Why is consistency more important than quantity?
4. ¿How can the Bible help with peer pressure?
5. ¿What book of the Bible will you start reading this week?

Action Step (This Week)

- Read one chapter of Proverbs each day.
- Write one verse that stood out to you.
- Pray before and after reading.

Prayer

Lord God, thank You for giving me Your Word. Teach me to understand it, love it, and obey it. Let Your truth guide my decisions and strengthen my faith every day. In Jesus' name. Amen.

Memory Verse

"All scripture is given by inspiration of God, and is profitable." — 2 Timothy 3:16

Chapter 4
Personal Notes

Use this space to write your thoughts, questions, key ideas, Scripture verses, insights, or practical applications from this chapter. Reflect on how the truths you are learning apply to your daily life, decisions, and relationships.

"Thy word is a lamp unto my feet, and a light unto my path." *(Psalm 119:105)*

____
____
____
____
____
____
____
____
____
____
____
____
____
____
____
____
____
____
____
____
____
____
____

Assignment Reflection (if applicable)

____

____

____

____

____

____

____

____

____

____

____

____

____

____

____

____

____

____

____

____

____

____

____

____

____

____

Date: _______________________________

Signature / Initials: _______________________________

CHAPTER 5

THE ASSEMBLY WITH BELIEVERS
Belonging, Growth, and Spiritual Protection

Key Verse

"Not forsaking the assembling of ourselves together, as the manner of some is; but exhorting one another." — Hebrews 10:25

Opening Thought

God never designed the Christian life to be lived alone. From the beginning, His plan has been to form a people — a spiritual family — where believers grow together, encourage one another, and walk in faith side by side.

Many teens believe in God but question the importance of church. This chapter explains why gathering with other believers is essential for spiritual growth, protection, and purpose.

Real Life Scenario — *"I Believe in God, But ¿Do I Need Church?"*

Jason is 15. He believes in God, reads his Bible sometimes, and prays when he feels stressed. But he rarely attends church. He tells his friends, *"Church isn't for me. I can worship God on my own."*

At first, Jason feels fine. But over time, his motivation fades. He stops reading Scripture regularly, struggles with temptation, and feels spiritually disconnected. Without realizing it, Jason is trying to grow spiritually without community. Jason's experience reflects a common misunderstanding among teens: believing that faith can survive without fellowship.

Big Truth
Faith grows stronger when we walk with other believers.

¿What is the Assembly of Believers?

The assembly of believers refers to Christians gathering together to worship God, learn His Word, pray, and encourage one another.

"For where two or three are gathered together in my name, there am I in the midst of them." — Matthew 18:20

The church is not merely a building—it is God's people united in Christ.

"Now ye are the body of Christ, and members in particular." — 1 Corinthians 12:27

¿Why Does God Want Us to Gather?

1. Because It Is God's Instruction: "Not forsaking the assembling of ourselves together." — Hebrews 10:25 - Gathering is not optional for spiritual growth.
2. Because We Need Encouragement: "Exhort one another daily." — Hebrews 3:13 - Faith is strengthened when believers support each other.
3. Because We Receive Spiritual Care: "For they watch for your souls." — Hebrews 13:17 - God uses pastors and leaders to protect and guide believers.

Church as a Spiritual Family

Just as a family provides care, correction, and support, the church provides spiritual nourishment and accountability.

"Now therefore ye are no more strangers and foreigners, but fellow citizens with the saints, and of the household of God." — Ephesians 2:19

In the church, believers:
- Learn together
- Worship together
- Grow together
- Serve together

¿What Happens When We Don't Gather?

When believers isolate themselves:
- Faith weakens
- Discouragement grows
- Temptation increases
- Spiritual confusion sets in

"Woe to him that is alone when he falleth." — Ecclesiastes 4:10

God never intended believers to fight spiritual battles alone.

Faith Meets Real Life

- **At School:** Church strengthens teens to stand firm in faith and values.
- **With Friends:** Christian friendships encourage wise decisions.
- **In Difficult Times:** Prayer and support from believers bring strength.
- **In Growth:** Accountability helps believers mature spiritually.

The Role of Youth Groups

Youth groups provide:
- Age-appropriate teaching
- Fellowship with peers
- Spiritual mentoring

"Let no man despise thy youth; but be thou an example of the believers." — 1 Timothy 4:12

Teens are not the future church—they are part of the church **now**.

Pastoral Warning

Choosing isolation weakens faith. While church is not perfect, God still uses it to shape, heal, and strengthen believers.

"Bear ye one another's burdens." — Galatians 6:2

Walking away from fellowship removes an important layer of spiritual protection.

Discussion Questions

1. ¿Why do some teens think church is unnecessary?
2. ¿How does fellowship strengthen faith?
3. ¿What are the dangers of spiritual isolation?
4. ¿How can youth group's help teens grow?
5. ¿How can you become more involved in your local church?

Action Step (This Week)

- Attend church or youth group faithfully this week.
- Introduce yourself to one new person.
- Pray for your pastor or youth leader.

Prayer

Lord God, thank You for giving me a spiritual family. Help me grow in community, walk in unity, and encourage others in faith. Teach me to value fellowship and remain faithful to Your Church. In Jesus' name. Amen.

Memory Verse

"For where two or three are gathered together in my name, there am I in the midst of them." — Matthew 18:20

Chapter 5
Personal Notes

Use this space to write your thoughts, questions, key ideas, Scripture verses, insights, or practical applications from this chapter. Reflect on how the truths you are learning apply to your daily life, decisions, and relationships.

"Thy word is a lamp unto my feet, and a light unto my path."
(Psalm 119:105)

____
____
____
____
____
____
____
____
____
____
____
____
____
____
____
____
____
____
____
____
____
____
____
____
____
____
____
____

Assignment Reflection (if applicable)

____

____

____

____

____

____

____

____

____

____

____

____

____

____

____

____

____

____

____

____

____

____

____

____

____

____

Date: _______________________________

Signature / Initials: _______________________________

CHAPTER 6

AUTHORITY IN THE CHURCH
Honor, Wisdom, and Healthy Spiritual Leadership

Key Verse

"Obey them that have the rule over you, and submit yourselves: for they watch for your souls." — Hebrews 13:17

Opening Thought

The word **authority** can make some teens uncomfortable. Many have seen authority misused at school, online, or even in churches. The Bible does not ignore this reality—but it also teaches that **healthy authority is God's design for protection, growth, and order**.

This chapter explains what biblical authority truly is, what it is not, and how teens can walk wisely under spiritual leadership while keeping a personal relationship with God.

Real Life Scenario — *"¿Can I Trust Church Leaders?"*

Ana is 14 years old. She loves God, but she struggles to trust leaders. She has heard stories online about pastors who failed morally or leaders who controlled people's lives. When her youth leader gives direction, Ana feels torn between respect and fear.

She wonders: *"What if authority is dangerous?"* *"How do I obey without being controlled?"*

Ana's questions are honest. The Bible gives clear answers that bring balance, wisdom, and peace.

Big Truth
Biblical authority exists to protect and serve—not to control.

¿What is authority according to the Bible?

The New Testament word for authority is **exousia**, meaning *delegated power* or *rightful responsibility*.

"For there is no power but of God: the powers that be are ordained of God." — Romans 13:1

This teaches us that:
- God is the highest authority
- All authority is delegated by Him
- Authority carries responsibility and accountability

¿Why did God establish authority?

God established authority to:
- Maintain order
- Provide spiritual protection
- Guide believers
- Correct in love

"For God is not the author of confusion, but of peace." — 1 Corinthians 14:33

Without authority, confusion and disorder grow. With healthy authority, peace and growth follow.

Jesus' Model of Authority

Jesus showed the true meaning of leadership.

"But whosoever will be great among you, let him be your minister." — Matthew 20:26

Jesus led by:
- Serving others
- Loving sacrificially
- Speaking truth
- Laying down His life

Biblical authority always follows **the example of Christ**.

Authority in the Local Church

God has placed spiritual leaders in the church to care for believers.

"And he gave some, apostles; and some, prophets; and some, evangelists; and some, pastors and teachers." — Ephesians 4:11

These leaders exist:

"For the perfecting of the saints... for the edifying of the body of Christ." — Ephesians 4:12

Their role is to build people up, not tear them down.

Obedience and Submission Explained

Obedience: Obedience means following godly instruction that aligns with Scripture. - "We ought to obey God rather than men." — Acts 5:29 - Obedience is **never blind**. God's Word is always the highest authority.

Submission: Submission is an attitude of respect, humility, and teachability.
- Obedience is an action
- Submission is a heart posture

Both are important for spiritual growth.

The Limits of Spiritual Authority

Biblical authority must never:
- Contradict Scripture
- Control personal decisions
- Replace your relationship with God
- Manipulate through fear or guilt

"For one is your Master, even Christ." — Matthew 23:10

All leaders answer to God.

Faith Meets Real Life

At Church: Respect leaders, listen carefully, and ask questions respectfully.
At Home: Honor parents and guardians. - "Honour thy father and thy mother." — Exodus 20:12
At School: Learning to respect authority builds maturity and character.
Online: Do not confuse loud voices with godly leadership.
Test everything by Scripture.

Healing From Past Hurt

Some teens have experienced hurt or disappointment from authority figures. God sees those wounds.

"He healeth the broken in heart." — Psalm 147:3

Healing comes through:
- Truth
- Forgiveness
- Healthy relationships
- God's Word

Pastoral Warning

Rejecting all authority because of bad experiences can isolate a believer and weaken faith. God calls us to **discernment**, not rebellion.

"Be ye followers of me, even as I also am of Christ." — 1 Corinthians 11:1

Discussion Questions

1. ¿What is biblical authority?
2. ¿How is God's authority different from control?
3. ¿What are the limits of spiritual authority?
4. ¿Why is submission an attitude of the heart?
5. ¿How can teens honor leaders while staying faithful to God?

Action Step (This Week)

- Pray for your pastor, youth leader, or spiritual mentor.
- Identify one authority God has placed in your life.
- Practice respectful communication this week.

Prayer

Lord God, teach me to walk under authority with wisdom and humility. Help me honor leaders while obeying Your Word first. Heal any wounds from the past and form in me a teachable heart. In Jesus' name. Amen.

Memory Verse: "Be ye followers of me, even as I also am of Christ." — 1 Corinthians 11:1

Use this space to write your thoughts, questions, key ideas, Scripture verses, insights, or practical applications from this chapter. Reflect on how the truths you are learning apply to your daily life, decisions, and relationships.

"Thy word is a lamp unto my feet, and a light unto my path." *(Psalm 119:105)*

____
____
____
____
____
____
____
____
____
____
____
____
____
____
____
____
____
____
____
____
____
____
____

Assignment Reflection (if applicable)

____

____

____

____

____

____

____

____

____

____

____

____

____

____

____

____

____

____

____

____

____

____

____

____

____

____

____

____

____

____

Date: _______________________

Signature / Initials: _______________________

CHAPTER 7
SERVANTS IN THE KINGDOM OF GOD
Purpose, Responsibility, and Serving Like Jesus

Key Verse

"For even the Son of man came not to be ministered unto, but to minister, and to give his life a ransom for many." — Mark 10:45

Opening Thought

In the world, greatness is often measured by popularity, power, or attention. In the Kingdom of God, greatness is measured differently. Jesus taught that true greatness is found in **serving others with humility and love**.

Many teens think serving God is something they will do "someday" when they are older. But Scripture teaches that **God calls and uses people at every age**. This chapter will help you understand that serving is not optional—it is part of who you are as a follower of Jesus.

Real Life Scenario — *"I'm Too Young to Serve"*

Miguel is 13 years old. He enjoys church, but when opportunities to serve are mentioned—helping with children, assisting in worship, or supporting church activities—he quietly steps back.

He thinks: *"I'm too young." "I don't know enough." "Serving is for adults."* Miguel doesn't realize that God often begins shaping servants early in life. Many biblical leaders were called while they were young.

Big Truth
Every believer is called to serve—no matter their age.

What Does It Mean to Serve in God's Kingdom?

To serve means to give your time, abilities, and heart to help others and honor God.

"As every man hath received the gift, even so minister the same one to another." — 1 Peter 4:10

Serving is not about position—it is about obedience.

Jesus: The Perfect Example of a Servant

Jesus showed us how to serve.

"I am among you as he that serveth." — Luke 22:27

Jesus:
- Served without seeking recognition
- Loved people sacrificially
- Obeyed the Father completely
- Put others before Himself

If Jesus served, so should we.

¿Why Does God Call Us to Serve?

1. Because Serving Builds Christlike Character: "Whosoever will be chief among you, let him be your servant." — Matthew 20:27 Serving produces humility, patience, and love.
2. Because God Gives Everyone Gifts: "For the body is not one member, but many." — 1 Corinthians 12:14 - No believer is useless in God's Kingdom.
3. Because We Will Give Account to God: "Moreover it is required in stewards, that a man be found faithful." — 1 Corinthians 4:2 - God measures faithfulness, not fame.

Serving Is Not Competition

The world compares; God calls.

"God hath set the members every one of them in the body, as it hath pleased him." — 1 Corinthians 12:18

Serving:
- Is not about being seen
- Is not about being better than others
- Is about being faithful where God places you

Where Can Teens Serve?

Teens can serve:
- In the local church
- In youth ministry
- At home
- At school
- In the community

"Whatsoever ye do, do it heartily, as to the Lord." — Colossians 3:23

Every act of service matters to God.

Faith Meets Real Life

- **At Church:** Serving connects you to the body of Christ.
- **At Home:** Helping family members is serving God.
- **At School:** Showing kindness and integrity is service.
- **With Friends:** Encouragement and prayer are powerful acts of service.

Common Excuses That Stop Teens from Serving

- "I'm too young" — God used Samuel and Timothy when they were young.
- "I'm not talented" — God gives gifts as He wills.
- "I'm afraid of failing" — Growth comes through obedience.

"Let no man despise thy youth." — 1 Timothy 4:12

Pastoral Warning

A believer who only receives but never serves will struggle to grow spiritually. Serving activates faith and deepens commitment.

"Faith without works is dead." — James 2:26

Discussion Questions

1. ¿What does it mean to serve in God's Kingdom?
2. ¿Why did Jesus emphasize serving?
3. ¿What excuses keep teens from serving?
4. ¿Where can you serve right now?
5. ¿How does serving help spiritual growth?

Action Step (This Week)

- Identify one way you can serve at church, home, or school.
- Volunteer once this week.
- Pray and ask God to show you where He wants you to serve.

Prayer

Lord Jesus, thank You for showing me the way of service. Teach me to serve with humility, love, and faithfulness. Show me where I can be useful in Your Kingdom and help me honor You with my life. Amen.

Memory Verse

"As every man hath received the gift, even so minister the same one to another." — 1 Peter 4:10

Chapter 7
Personal Notes

Use this space to write your thoughts, questions, key ideas, Scripture verses, insights, or practical applications from this chapter. Reflect on how the truths you are learning apply to your daily life, decisions, and relationships.

"Thy word is a lamp unto my feet, and a light unto my path." *(Psalm 119:105)*

Assignment Reflection (if applicable)

____

____

____

____

____

____

____

____

____

____

____

____

____

____

____

____

____

____

____

____

____

____

____

____

____

____

____

Date: _______________________________

Signature / Initials: _______________________________

CHAPTER 8

PRAYER
Living in Daily Communion with God

Key Verse

"Call unto me, and I will answer thee, and shew thee great and mighty things, which thou knowest not." — Jeremiah 33:3

Opening Thought

Prayer is not a performance, a speech, or a religious routine. Prayer is **relationship**. Just as friendships grow through conversation, our relationship with God grows when we talk with Him and learn to listen to Him.

Many teens believe prayer is important, yet feel unsure how to pray or what to say. This chapter will help you understand prayer in a simple, honest, and biblical way—so prayer becomes part of everyday life, not just a last resort.

Real Life Scenario — *"I Don't Know How to Pray"*

Jordan is 14 years old. He believes in God and wants to pray, but every time he tries, his mind wanders. He starts strong—then feels awkward, distracted, or unsure if God is even listening.

He thinks: *"¿What if I'm praying the wrong way?" "¿Why does prayer feel easier for other people?"*

Jordan eventually stops praying regularly—not because he doesn't believe, but because he doesn't understand prayer. Many teens feel the same way.

Big Truth
Prayer is simply talking with God and trusting Him to listen.

¿What Is Prayer?

Prayer is communication with God that includes:
- Worship
- Thanksgiving
- Confession
- Requests
- Listening

"Let us therefore come boldly unto the throne of grace." — Hebrews 4:16

Prayer is not about impressing God with words. It is about approaching Him with honesty and faith.

¿Why Should We Pray?

1. Because God Invites Us to Pray: "Call unto me, and I will answer thee." — Jeremiah 33:3 - Prayer is an invitation, not an obligation.
2. Because We Depend on God: "Without me ye can do nothing." — John 15:5 - Prayer reminds us that we are not self-sufficient.
3. Because Prayer Builds Relationship: "Draw nigh to God, and he will draw nigh to you." — James 4:8

¿When Should We Pray?

The Bible teaches that prayer should be continual.

"Pray without ceasing." — 1 Thessalonians 5:17

We can pray:

- In the morning
- During the day
- Before decisions
- In moments of stress
- In joy and gratitude

Prayer fits into real life.

¿How did Jesus teach us to pray?

Jesus gave His disciples a clear model.

"After this manner therefore pray ye." — Matthew 6:9

The Lord's Prayer Explained

1. **"Our Father which art in heaven"**: Prayer begins with relationship. God is a loving Father.
2. **"Hallowed be thy name"**: We honor and worship God.
3. **"Thy kingdom come"**: We invite God's will into our lives.
4. **"Thy will be done"**: Prayer includes surrender.
5. **"Give us this day our daily bread"**: We bring our needs to God.
6. **"Forgive us our debts"**: Prayer includes repentance and forgiveness.
7. **"Lead us not into temptation"**: We ask for strength and guidance.
8. **"Deliver us from evil"**: We depend on God's protection.
9. **"For thine is the kingdom"**: Prayer ends with confidence and praise.

¿Does God Always Answer Prayer?

Yes—but not always the way we expect.

God's answers may be:
- **Yes**
- **No**
- **Wait**

"And this is the confidence that we have in him, that, if we ask any thing according to his will, he heareth us." — 1 John 5:14

God answers according to His wisdom and love.

Faith Meets Real Life

- **When You Feel Stressed:** Prayer brings peace. "Be careful for nothing; but in every thing by prayer…" — Philippians 4:6–7
- **When You Feel Tempted:** Prayer brings strength.
- **When You Feel Lonely:** Prayer brings God's presence.
- **When You Feel Thankful:** Prayer becomes praise.

Common Obstacles to Prayer

- Distraction
- Feeling unworthy
- Lack of routine
- Unrealistic expectations

God does not expect perfect prayers—He desires sincere hearts.

Building a Daily Prayer Habit

Simple steps:

- Choose a quiet place
- Set a regular time
- Start with honesty
- Use Scripture in prayer

"The effectual fervent prayer of a righteous man availeth much."
— James 5:16

Pastoral Warning

Neglecting prayer weakens spiritual sensitivity. A prayerless life slowly becomes a powerless life.

"Watch and pray, that ye enter not into temptation." — Matthew 26:41

Discussion Questions

1. ¿Why do many teens struggle with prayer?
2. ¿What does it mean that prayer is relationship, not performance?
3. ¿How did Jesus model prayer?
4. ¿What distractions affect your prayer life?
5. ¿How can prayer help in daily challenges?

Action Step (This Week)

- Pray for 5 minutes each day this week.
- Write one prayer request and one thank-you.
- Try praying using the Lord's Prayer as a guide.

Prayer

Heavenly Father, thank You for inviting me to talk with You. Teach me to pray honestly and consistently. Help me trust You with my needs, fears, and future. Draw me closer to You each day. In Jesus' name. Amen.

Use this space to write your thoughts, questions, key ideas, Scripture verses, insights, or practical applications from this chapter. Reflect on how the truths you are learning apply to your daily life, decisions, and relationships.

"Thy word is a lamp unto my feet, and a light unto my path." *(Psalm 119:105)*

____
____
____
____
____
____
____
____
____
____
____
____
____
____
____
____
____
____
____
____
____
____
____

Assignment Reflection (if applicable)

____

____

____

____

____

____

____

____

____

____

____

____

____

____

____

____

____

____

____

____

____

____

____

____

____

____

____

Date: _______________________________

Signature / Initials: _______________________________

CHAPTER 9
WORSHIP: LIVING FOR GOD'S GLORY
More Than Music—A Lifestyle of Surrender

Key Verse

"I beseech you therefore, brethren, by the mercies of God, that ye present your bodies a living sacrifice, holy, acceptable unto God, which is your reasonable service." — Romans 12:1

Opening Thought

When many teens hear the word *worship*, they think of music, singing, or a moment during a church service. While music can be part of worship, the Bible teaches that worship is **much more than a song**. Worship is how we live every day in response to who God is.

This chapter will help you understand worship as a lifestyle—one that honors God with choices, attitudes, and obedience.

Real Life Scenario — *"I Worship at Church… But Not Always at School"*

Alyssa is 15. She loves worship music and sings passionately during youth services. But during the week at school, she struggles. When friends pressure her to gossip, cheat on homework, or post unkind comments online, she often goes along.

Later, Alyssa feels conflicted. She wonders: *"¿Why does worship feel real at church but not in my everyday life?"*

Alyssa's struggle reveals a common misunderstanding: thinking worship is limited to a place or a moment instead of a daily way of living.

Big Truth
Worship is how I live, not just what I sing.

¿What Is Worship According to the Bible?

The Bible describes worship as honoring God with reverence, love, and obedience.

"God is a Spirit: and they that worship him must worship him in spirit and in truth." — John 4:24

To worship God means:
- To recognize His greatness
- To submit our will to His will
- To live in obedience to His Word

Worship flows from a heart that belongs to God.

Worship Begins With Surrender

True worship starts when we surrender ourselves to God.

"Present your bodies a living sacrifice." — Romans 12:1

A *living sacrifice* means:
- Choosing God's way over our own
- Saying no to sin
- Saying yes to obedience

Surrender is not weakness—it is trust.

Jesus: Our Example of Worship

Jesus lived a life of perfect worship.

"I seek not mine own will, but the will of the Father which hath sent me." — John 5:30

Jesus worshiped the Father by:
- Obeying Him completely
- Loving people sacrificially
- Living with humility

If Jesus worshiped through obedience, so should we.

Worship and Daily Choices

Worship shows up in everyday decisions:
- How you speak to others
- How you treat your family
- What you watch and listen to
- How you use social media
- How you respond to temptation

"Whether therefore ye eat, or drink, or whatsoever ye do, do all to the glory of God." — 1 Corinthians 10:31

Every choice can honor God.

Faith Meets Real Life

- **At School:** Choosing honesty and kindness is worship.
- **With Friends:** Standing for what is right honors God.
- **Online:** Posting with integrity reflects worship.
- **In Private:** Obedience when no one is watching is true worship.

Music and Worship

Music is a powerful expression of worship.

"Speaking to yourselves in psalms and hymns and spiritual songs." — Ephesians 5:19

However, music without obedience becomes empty.

"This people draweth nigh unto me with their mouth… but their heart is far from me." — Matthew 15:8

God desires hearts surrendered—not just voices raised.

Worship Shapes Identity

What we worship shapes who we become.

When we worship:

- Our minds are renewed
- Our hearts are aligned with God
- Our character is transformed

"But we all… beholding as in a glass the glory of the Lord, are changed into the same image." — 2 Corinthians 3:18

Pastoral Warning

It is possible to sing worship songs while living in disobedience. God calls us to consistent worship—public and private.

"If ye love me, keep my commandments." — John 14:15

Discussion Questions

1. ¿How do most people define worship?
2. ¿Why is worship more than music?
3. ¿How does obedience relate to worship?
4. ¿What areas of daily life can become acts of worship?
5. ¿How can worship shape your identity?

Action Step (This Week)

- Choose one daily habit to offer to God as worship.
- Before making decisions, ask: *Does this honor God?*
- Listen to worship music and apply the message through obedience.

Prayer

Lord God, I give You my life as worship. Teach me to honor You not only with my words, but with my choices and actions. Help me live surrendered and obedient to Your will. May my life bring You glory every day. Amen.

Memory Verse

"Whether therefore ye eat, or drink, or whatsoever ye do, do all to the glory of God." — 1 Corinthians 10:31

Use this space to write your thoughts, questions, key ideas, Scripture verses, insights, or practical applications from this chapter. Reflect on how the truths you are learning apply to your daily life, decisions, and relationships.

"Thy word is a lamp unto my feet, and a light unto my path." *(Psalm 119:105)*

Assignment Reflection (if applicable)

____

____

____

____

____

____

____

____

____

____

____

____

____

____

____

____

____

____

____

____

____

____

____

____

Date: _______________________________

Signature / Initials: _______________________________

CHAPTER 10
PRAISE: CELEBRATING THE WORKS OF GOD
Living With Gratitude, Joy, and Victory

Key Verse

"I will bless the LORD at all times: his praise shall continually be in my mouth." — Psalm 34:1

Opening Thought

Praise is a joyful response to what God has done, is doing, and will do. While worship focuses on **WHO GOD IS**, praise celebrates **what God does**. Praise lifts our eyes above circumstances and reminds us that God is faithful, powerful, and present.

For many teens, praise feels easy when life is good—but difficult when life is painful. This chapter will help you understand that praise is not based on feelings, but on faith.

Real Life Scenario — *"¿How Can I Praise God When Life Is Hard?"*

Daniel is 15. His parents are going through a difficult season, his grades are slipping, and he feels overwhelmed. At church, others raise their hands and sing joyfully, but Daniel stands quietly, feeling disconnected.

He wonders: *"¿How can I praise God when nothing feels right?"*

Daniel's question reflects a struggle many teens face—learning to praise God not only in victories, but also in trials.

Big Truth
Praise declares God's goodness even when circumstances are difficult.

¿What Is Praise?

Praise is the verbal and visible expression of gratitude, honor, and celebration toward God.

"Praise him for his mighty acts." — Psalm 150:2

Praise includes:
- Speaking God's goodness
- Singing joyfully
- Thanking God publicly
- Testifying of His works

Praise shifts our focus from problems to God's power.

¿Why should we praise God?

1. Because God Commands It: "Let every thing that hath breath praise the LORD." — Psalm 150:6 - Praise is not optional—it is part of our calling.

2. Because We Were Created for God's Glory: "For thou hast created all things, and for thy pleasure they are and were created." — Revelation 4:11 - Praise aligns our lives with our purpose.

3. Because Praise Invites God's Presence: "But thou art holy, O thou that inhabitest the praises of Israel." — Psalm 22:3 - Praise creates an atmosphere where God's presence is welcomed.

The Power of Praise in the Bible
Paul and Silas in Prison

"And at midnight Paul and Silas prayed, and sang praises unto God: and the prisoners heard them. And suddenly there was a great earthquake, so that the foundations of the prison were shaken: and immediately all the doors were opened, and every one's bands were loosed." — Acts 16:25 - Praise in the middle of suffering led to freedom.

King Jehoshaphat's Battle

"When they began to sing and to praise, the LORD set ambushments." — 2 Chronicles 20:22

Praise preceded victory.

These examples teach us that praise is powerful spiritual warfare.

Praise Is a Choice

Praise is not based on emotions.

"In every thing give thanks." — 1 Thessalonians 5:18

Choosing praise:
- Strengthens faith
- Defeats discouragement
- Builds spiritual resilience

Praise does not deny pain—it declares trust in God.

Faith Meets Real Life

- **When You Feel Discouraged:** Praise lifts your spirit.
- **When You Feel Afraid:** Praise reminds you of God's power.
- **When You Feel Grateful:** Praise expresses thanksgiving.
- **When You Feel Weak:** Praise invites God's strength.

Praise and Testimony

Praise often becomes testimony. - "Let the redeemed of the LORD say so." — Psalm 107:2 - Sharing what God has done encourages others and strengthens your own faith.

Pastoral Warning

Complaining weakens faith, while praise strengthens it.

"Do all things without murmurings and disputings." — Philippians 2:14

Praise guards the heart against bitterness and unbelief.

Discussion Questions

1. ¿What is the difference between worship and praise?
2. ¿Why is praise difficult during hard seasons?
3. ¿What biblical examples show the power of praise?
4. ¿How does praise affect our attitude?
5. ¿How can praise become a daily habit?

Action Step (This Week)

- Begin each day by thanking God for three things.
- Praise God verbally, even when you don't feel like it.
- Share one testimony of God's goodness with someone this week.

Prayer

Lord God, I choose to praise You at all times. Help me trust You in every season—good or difficult. Fill my heart with gratitude, joy, and faith. May my praise glorify You and strengthen my walk with You. Amen.

Memory Verse

"I will bless the LORD at all times: his praise shall continually be in my mouth." — Psalm 34:1

Use this space to write your thoughts, questions, key ideas, Scripture verses, insights, or practical applications from this chapter. Reflect on how the truths you are learning apply to your daily life, decisions, and relationships.

"Thy word is a lamp unto my feet, and a light unto my path." *(Psalm 119:105)*

Assignment Reflection (if applicable)

____

____

____

____

____

____

____

____

____

____

____

____

____

____

____

____

____

____

____

____

____

____

____

____

____

____

____

Date: _______________________________

Signature / Initials: _______________________________

CHAPTER 11
STEWARDSHIP: HONORING GOD WITH OUR RESOURCES
Faithful Living With What God Entrusts to Us

Key Verse

"Moreover it is required in stewards, that a man be found faithful." — 1 Corinthians 4:2

Opening Thought

Stewardship is not only about money. Stewardship is about **faithfully managing everything God has entrusted to us**—our time, abilities, relationships, influence, and resources. God does not ask us to be rich or perfect; He asks us to be faithful.

Many teens believe stewardship is an "adult topic," but Scripture teaches that learning faithfulness early shapes a strong and responsible Christian life.

Real Life Scenario — *"¿It's mine… Right?"*

Sofia is 14. She receives a small allowance and recently got her first phone. She enjoys spending money on snacks, games, and subscriptions. When her youth leader talks about honoring God with resources, Sofia quietly thinks:

"It's my money. I earned it. Why should God care how I use it?"

Sofia's question is honest—and important. Stewardship begins with understanding **who truly owns everything**.

Big Truth
Everything I have belongs to God, and I am called to manage it faithfully.

¿What is Biblical Stewardship?

A steward is someone who manages what belongs to another.

"The earth is the LORD'S, and the fullness thereof." — Psalm 24:1

Biblical stewardship means:
- Recognizing God as the owner
- Managing resources wisely
- Using what we have to honor God

We are managers—not owners.

¿Why Does God Care About Stewardship?

1. Stewardship Reveals the Heart: "For where your treasure is, there will your heart be also." — Matthew 6:21 - How we use our resources shows what we value.
2. Stewardship Prepares Us for Greater Responsibility: "He that is faithful in that which is least is faithful also in much." — Luke 16:10 - God often tests faithfulness in small things before entrusting bigger things.
3. Stewardship Honors God: "Honour the LORD with thy substance." — Proverbs 3:9 - Faithful stewardship is an act of worship.

¿What Resources Has God Given Teens?

God entrusts teens with:
- **Time** — how you spend your days
- **Talents** — skills and abilities
- **Finances** — money, gifts, allowances
- **Relationships** — family and friends
- **Influence** — words, actions, online presence

"As every man hath received the gift, even so minister the same one to another." — 1 Peter 4:10

Stewardship of Time

Time is one of the most valuable resources God gives.

"Redeeming the time, because the days are evil." — Ephesians 5:16

Faithful use of time includes:
- Prioritizing God
- Balancing responsibilities
- Avoiding constant distractions

Stewardship of Finances

Money itself is not evil—but loving money more than God is dangerous.

"For the love of money is the root of all evil." — 1 Timothy 6:10

Biblical principles include:
- Giving with gratitude
- Spending wisely
- Avoiding greed
- Learning generosity early

"God loveth a cheerful giver." — 2 Corinthians 9:7

Stewardship of Talents and Gifts

God gives abilities for a purpose.

"For we are his workmanship, created in Christ Jesus unto good works." — Ephesians 2:10

Talents may include:
- Music
- Leadership
- Creativity
- Helping others
- Learning and teaching

Using gifts for God brings joy and growth.

Faith Meets Real Life

- **At School:** Managing time, studies, and integrity honors God.
- **At Home:** Helping responsibly is stewardship.
- **Online:** Using influence wisely reflects faithfulness.
- **With Money:** Choosing generosity over impulse builds character.

The Danger of Poor Stewardship

Poor stewardship leads to:
- Waste
- Selfishness
- Spiritual immaturity

"Take heed, and beware of covetousness." — Luke 12:15

God calls us to wisdom, not excess.

Pastoral Warning

Faithfulness does not mean perfection. It means obedience, learning, and growth. God is patient and teaches us as we mature.

"His lord said unto him, Well done, thou good and faithful servant." — Matthew 25:21

Discussion Questions

1. ¿What does stewardship mean?
2. ¿Why does God care how we use our resources?
3. ¿What resources has God given teens?
4. ¿How can stewardship be an act of worship?
5. ¿What area of stewardship do you need to improve?

Action Step (This Week)

- Track how you spend your time for one week.
- Set aside something (time or money) to give generously.
- Pray before spending or posting online.

Prayer

Lord God, thank You for everything You have given me. Teach me to be faithful with my time, talents, and resources. Help me honor You with my choices and grow in wisdom and responsibility. Amen.

Memory Verse

"Moreover it is required in stewards, that a man be found faithful." — 1 Corinthians 4:2

Use this space to write your thoughts, questions, key ideas, Scripture verses, insights, or practical applications from this chapter. Reflect on how the truths you are learning apply to your daily life, decisions, and relationships.

"Thy word is a lamp unto my feet, and a light unto my path." (Psalm 119:105)

Assignment Reflection (if applicable)

____ 90
____
____
____
____
____
____
____
____
____
____
____
____
____
____
____
____
____
____
____
____
____
____
____
____
____
____
____

Date: ______________________________
Signature / Initials: ______________________________

CHAPTER 12

THE FRUIT OF THE HOLY SPIRIT
A Transformed Life That Reflects Christ

Key Verse

"But the fruit of the Spirit is love, joy, peace, longsuffering, gentleness, goodness, faith, Meekness, temperance: against such there is no law." — Galatians 5:22–23

Opening Thought

God's goal for every believer is not only salvation, but **transformation**. While gifts show what we can do, fruit shows **who we are becoming**. The Holy Spirit works within us to form the character of Christ in our daily lives.

For teens, character is shaped early—through choices, habits, friendships, and responses to pressure. This chapter will help you understand how the Holy Spirit produces fruit in you and how that fruit changes the way you live.

Real Life Scenario — *"I Believe in God, but I Still Lose My Temper"*

Carlos is 15. He loves God and attends youth group regularly. Yet at home and school, he struggles with anger and impatience. When things don't go his way, he reacts quickly and later feels regret.

He asks himself: *"If the Holy Spirit lives in me, ¿why do I still struggle?"* Carlos's question is honest. Growth in Christ is a **process**, and the fruit of the Spirit develops over time.

Big Truth
The Holy Spirit transforms my character as I walk with Him daily.

¿What is the Fruit of the Holy Spirit?

The fruit of the Spirit is the visible evidence of God's work inside a believer.

"Ye shall know them by their fruits." — Matthew 7:16

Notice that Scripture speaks of **one fruit** with many expressions—not separate fruits. The Holy Spirit produces a complete, Christlike character.

¿Why Does God Desire Fruit in Our Lives?

1. Fruit Reflects God's Character: "Be ye therefore perfect, even as your Father which is in heaven is perfect." — Matthew 5:48 - God desires His children to reflect His nature.
2. Fruit Glorifies God: "Herein is my Father glorified, that ye bear much fruit." — John 15:8 - A transformed life points others to Christ.
3. Fruit Shows Spiritual Maturity: "Strong meat belongeth to them that are of full age." — Hebrews 5:14 - Maturity is measured by character, not popularity.

The Nine Expressions of the Fruit of the Spirit

1. Love: Choosing to care for others selflessly. "By this shall all men know that ye are my disciples." (John 13:35)
2. Joy: Deep gladness rooted in God, not circumstances. "The joy of the LORD is your strength." (Nehemiah 8:10)
3. Peace: Inner calm that comes from trusting God. "And the peace of God... shall keep your hearts." (Philippians 4:7)
4. Longsuffering: Patience with people and situations. "Charity suffereth long." (1 Corinthians 13:4)

5. Gentleness: Kindness expressed through words and actions. "Be ye kind one to another." (Ephesians 4:32)

6. Goodness: Choosing what is right even when it is difficult. "Abhor that which is evil; cleave to that which is good." (Romans 12:9)

7. Faith: Faithfulness, reliability, and trust in God. "It is required in stewards, that a man be found faithful." (1 Corinthians 4:2)

8. Meekness: Strength under control. "Blessed are the meek." (Matthew 5:5)

9. Temperance: Self-control over desires and emotions. "He that is slow to anger is better than the mighty." (Proverbs 16:32)

¿How is the Fruit of the spirit developed?

Fruit grows by **abiding in Christ**.

"I am the vine, ye are the branches." — John 15:5

The fruit develops as we:
- Spend time in prayer
- Study God's Word
- Obey the Holy Spirit
- Allow correction
- Practice godly habits

Fruit cannot be forced—it is produced through relationship.

Fruit vs. Gifts

- **Gifts** are given instantly
- **Fruit** develops gradually

"Though I speak with the tongues of men and of angels, and have not charity, I am nothing." — 1 Corinthians 13:1

God values character more than ability.

Faith Meets Real Life

- **At Home:** Responding with patience shows fruit.
- **At School:** Choosing kindness reflects Christ.
- **With Friends:** Self-control honors God.
- **Online:** Gentleness and wisdom display maturity.

Pastoral Warning

Spiritual growth takes time. Do not be discouraged by struggle.

Stay connected to Christ and allow the Holy Spirit to continue His work.

"Being confident of this very thing, that he which hath begun a good work in you will perform it." — Philippians 1:6

Discussion Questions

1. ¿What is the fruit of the Holy Spirit?
2. ¿Why is fruit more important than gifts?
3. ¿Which areas of the fruit are strongest in your life?
4. ¿Which areas need growth?
5. ¿How can teens cooperate with the Holy Spirit daily?

Action Step (This Week)

- Choose one area of the fruit to practice intentionally.
- Pray daily for the Holy Spirit's help.
- Reflect on how your reactions show spiritual growth.

Prayer

Holy Spirit, thank You for living within me. Transform my heart and shape my character. Help me grow in love, patience, self-control, and faithfulness. May my life reflect Jesus Christ in every area. Amen.

Memory Verse

"But the fruit of the Spirit is love, joy, peace, longsuffering, gentleness, goodness, faith. Meekness, temperance: against such there is no law.

— Galatians 5:22-23

PERSONAL NOTES & ASSIGNMENT REFLECTION
Chapter 12
Personal Notes

Use this space to write your thoughts, questions, key ideas, Scripture verses, insights, or practical applications from this chapter. Reflect on how the truths you are learning apply to your daily life, decisions, and relationships.

"Thy word is a lamp unto my feet, and a light unto my path." (Psalm 119:105)

____

____

____

____

____

____

____

____

____

____

____

____

____

____

____

____

____

____

____

____

____

____

____

____

____

____

____

____

Date: _______________________________

Signature / Initials: _______________________________

CHAPTER 13

SPIRITUAL GIFTS: EQUIPPED TO SERVE
Discovering, Developing, and Using God's Gifts With Wisdom

Key Verse

"But the manifestation of the Spirit is given to every man to profit withal." — 1 Corinthians 12:7

Opening Thought

God not only transforms our character through the fruit of the Holy Spirit; He also **empowers us to serve** through spiritual gifts. These gifts are not rewards for maturity nor signs of spiritual superiority. They are gracious empowerments given by God to build up others and strengthen the Church.

For teens, understanding spiritual gifts early helps prevent confusion, pride, fear, and misuse. This chapter will guide you to recognize God's gifts, understand their purpose, and use them with humility and love.

Real Life Scenario — *"¿Do I Have a Spiritual Gift?"*

Nathan is 15. He watches others at church preach, sing, pray boldly, or serve confidently. He quietly wonders:

"I love God, but ¿do I have a spiritual gift?" "¿What if I don't have anything special to offer?"

Nathan's questions are common. The Bible clearly teaches that **every believer receives gifts from the Holy Spirit**—including teens.

Big Truth
God gives spiritual gifts to every believer to serve others and glorify Christ.

¿What Are Spiritual Gifts?

Spiritual gifts are special abilities given by the Holy Spirit to believers for ministry and service.

"Now there are diversities of gifts, but the same Spirit." — 1 Corinthians 12:4

Spiritual gifts:
- Come from God
- Are given by grace
- Are meant to help others
- Must align with Scripture

They are not earned, chosen, or manufactured.

¿Why Does God Give Spiritual Gifts?

1. To Build Up the Church: "Let all things be done unto edifying." — 1 Corinthians 14:26 - Gifts exist to strengthen the body of Christ.
2. To Serve Others: "As every man hath received the gift, even so minister the same one to another." — 1 Peter 4:10 - Gifts are tools for love and service.
3. To Glorify God: "That God in all things may be glorified." — 1 Peter 4:11 - Gifts point to God—not to ourselves.

The Personal (Manifestational) Gifts of the Holy Spirit

The Bible identifies **nine personal gifts** (1 Corinthians 12:8–10), commonly grouped into three categories.

Gifts of Revelation

- **Word of Wisdom** — God-given insight for direction
- **Word of Knowledge** — Revealed information for edification
- **Discerning of Spirits** — Recognizing spiritual sources

Gifts of Inspiration

- **Prophecy** — Supernatural ability to see the future with the intention to edify, comfort or give exhortation to the church.
- **Divers Kinds of Tongues** — Supernatural ability to pray or give messages in other languages.
- **Interpretation of Tongues** — Supernatural ability to interpret meaning of what was said in tongues.

Gifts of Power

- **Faith** — Supernatural confidence in God
- **Gifts of Healing** — God's healing work
- **Working of Miracles** — Manifestations of divine power

"All these worketh that one and the selfsame Spirit." — 1 Corinthians 12:11

Ministerial Gifts

Beyond personal gifts, Scripture identifies **ministerial gifts** given to the Church:

"And he gave some, apostles; and some, prophets; and some, evangelists; and some, pastors and teachers." — Ephesians 4:11

These gifts exist: "For the perfecting of the saints, for the work of the ministry." — Ephesians 4:12

Ministerial gifts develop over time through calling, training, and character.

Order, Love, and Maturity

Spiritual gifts must operate with love and order.

"The spirits of the prophets are subject to the prophets." — 1 Corinthians 14:32

"Though I speak with the tongues of men and of angels, and have not charity, I am nothing." — 1 Corinthians 13:1

Love governs the use of gifts.

¿How Do I Discover My Spiritual Gifts?

1. **Stay close to God** through prayer and the Word
2. **Serve faithfully** in small opportunities
3. **Seek godly counsel**
4. **Observe fruit** and confirmation

God reveals gifts as we walk obediently.

Faith Meets Real Life

- **At Church:** Serving with gifts strengthens others.
- **At School:** Wisdom, faith, and discernment guide decisions.
- **With Friends:** Encouragement and prayer reflect gifting.
- **In the Future:** God develops gifts for lifelong service.

Pastoral Warning

Gifts without character can harm the Church. Fruit must always guide gifts.

"By their fruits ye shall know them." — Matthew 7:20

God seeks humility, obedience, and love.

Discussion Questions

1. ¿What are spiritual gifts?
2. ¿Why does God give gifts to every believer?
3. ¿What is the difference between gifts and fruit?
4. ¿Why are love and order important?
5. ¿How can teens begin discovering their gifts?

Action Step (This Week)

- Pray and ask God to reveal your gifts.
- Serve in one area at church or home.
- Write down where you see God using you.

Prayer

Holy Spirit, thank You for equipping me to serve. Help me use Your gifts with humility and love. Teach me to serve others faithfully and bring glory to Jesus Christ. Amen.

Memory Verse

"But the manifestation of the Spirit is given to every man to profit withal." — 1 Corinthians 12:7

Use this space to write your thoughts, questions, key ideas, Scripture verses, insights, or practical applications from this chapter. Reflect on how the truths you are learning apply to your daily life, decisions, and relationships.

"Thy word is a lamp unto my feet, and a light unto my path." *(Psalm 119:105)*

Assignment Reflection (if applicable)

____

____

____

____

____

____

____

____

____

____

____

____

____

____

____

____

____

____

____

____

____

____

____

____

____

____

____

____

Date: ________________________________

Signature / Initials: ____________________________________

CHAPTER 14
EVANGELISM: SHARING YOUR FAITH WITH LOVE AND TRUTH
Being a Witness for Christ in Everyday Life

Key Verse

"But ye shall receive power, after that the Holy Ghost is come upon you: and ye shall be witnesses unto me…" — Acts 1:8

Opening Thought

Evangelism is not only for pastors, missionaries, or adults. Evangelism is the calling of **every believer**, including teens. To evangelize means to share the good news of Jesus Christ through words, actions, and lifestyle.

Many teens feel nervous or unprepared to talk about their faith. This chapter will help you understand that evangelism is not about arguing or pressuring others, but about **loving people and pointing them to Jesus**.

Real Life Scenario — *"¿What If They Laugh at Me?"*

Emily is 14. She loves Jesus, but at school she keeps her faith quiet. When conversations turn to faith or church, she stays silent. She thinks: *"¿What if they make fun of me?" "¿What if I say the wrong thing?"*

Emily wants to share her faith but fears rejection. Many teens struggle with the same fear, yet God calls us to courage rooted in love.

Big Truth
I share my faith because Jesus changed my life, and others need His love.

¿What is Evangelism?

Evangelism means sharing the Gospel—the good news that Jesus Christ saves, forgives, and gives eternal life.

"For God so loved the world, that he gave his only begotten Son." — John 3:16

Evangelism includes:
- Sharing what Jesus has done
- Living a Christlike life
- Inviting others to know Him

¿Why Should We Evangelize?

1. Because Jesus Commanded It: "Go ye into all the world, and preach the gospel." — Mark 16:15 - Evangelism is obedience.
2. Because People Need Salvation: "For all have sinned, and come short of the glory of God." — Romans 3:23 - Without Christ, people remain separated from God.
3. Because We Are Ambassadors for Christ: "Now then we are ambassadors for Christ." — 2 Corinthians 5:20 - God represents Himself through His people.

¿What is the Gospel Message?

The Gospel can be explained simply:
1. God loves us
2. Sin separates us from God
3. Jesus died and rose again
4. Salvation is received by faith

"That if thou shalt confess with thy mouth the Lord Jesus... thou shalt be saved." — Romans 10:9

¿How Can Teens Share Their Faith?

1. Through Your Testimony: "Let the redeemed of the LORD say so." — Psalm 107:2 - Your story matters.
2. Through Your Lifestyle: "Let your light so shine before men." — Matthew 5:16 - Kindness, honesty, and integrity speak loudly.
3. Through Words: "Be ready always to give an answer." — 1 Peter 3:15 - Speak with gentleness and respect.
4. Through Invitation: Inviting friends to church or youth group is evangelism.

Faith Meets Real Life

- **At School:** Standing for truth with respect is evangelism.
- **With Friends:** Listening and praying opens hearts.
- **Online:** Sharing hope and encouragement reflects Christ.
- **In the Community:** Serving others shows God's love.

Evangelism and the Holy Spirit

We do not evangelize alone.

"Not by might, nor by power, but by my spirit, saith the LORD." — Zechariah 4:6

The Holy Spirit:
- Gives boldness
- Convicts hearts
- Guides conversations

Pastoral Warning

Evangelism should never be forceful or argumentative. "Speaking the truth in love." — Ephesians 4:15 - Our goal is not to win arguments, but to win hearts.

Discussion Questions

1. ¿What is evangelism?
2. ¿Why do teens fear sharing their faith?
3. ¿How can lifestyle be a form of evangelism?
4. ¿What role does the Holy Spirit play?
5. ¿Who can you pray for this week?

Action Step (This Week)

- Pray for one person who does not know Jesus.
- Share one encouraging Scripture or testimony.
- Invite a friend to church or youth group.

Prayer

Lord Jesus, thank You for saving me. Give me courage, love, and wisdom to share my faith with others.¿ Use my words and my life to point people to You. Amen.

Memory Verse

"Ye shall be witnesses unto me." — Acts 1:8

Use this space to write your thoughts, questions, key ideas, Scripture verses, insights, or practical applications from this chapter. Reflect on how the truths you are learning apply to your daily life, decisions, and relationships.

"Thy word is a lamp unto my feet, and a light unto my path." *(Psalm 119:105)*

Assignment Reflection (if applicable)

____

____

____

____

____

____

____

____

____

____

____

____

____

____

____

____

____

____

____

____

____

____

____

____

____

____

____

____

____

Date: _______________________________

Signature / Initials: _______________________________

CHAPTER 15
HEAVEN AND HELL: AN ETERNAL DECISION
Choosing Life, Hope, and Eternity With God

Key Verse

"And as it is appointed unto men once to die, but after this the judgment." — Hebrews 9:27

Opening Thought

Every person will live forever. The Bible teaches that life does not end at death—**it transitions into eternity**. The most important question is not how long we live on earth, but **where we will spend eternity**.

This chapter presents biblical truth with clarity, love, and seriousness. God does not want anyone to live in fear, but He does want us to understand the eternal significance of our choices.

Real Life Scenario — *"¿What Happens After We Die?"*

Lucas is 15. After attending a funeral for the first time, he feels unsettled. That night, questions fill his mind: *"¿Is heaven real?"* *"¿What happens to people who don't believe?"* *"¿How can I be sure where I will go?"*

These questions are not signs of weakness—they are signs of maturity. God invites us to seek truth about eternity.

Big Truth
What I decide about Jesus determines where I will spend eternity.

¿What does the Bible Teach about Eternity?

Scripture clearly teaches that human beings are eternal.

"Then shall the dust return to the earth as it was: and the spirit shall return unto God who gave it." — Ecclesiastes 12:7

Life on earth is temporary; eternity is permanent.

¿What is Heaven?

Heaven is the eternal dwelling place of God, prepared for those who believe in Jesus Christ.

"In my Father's house are many mansions... I go to prepare a place for you." — John 14:2

Heaven is:
- A real place
- Free from pain, sorrow, and death
- Filled with God's presence
- A place of joy and peace

"And God shall wipe away all tears from their eyes." — Revelation 21:4

¿Who Will Enter Heaven?

Jesus made the way clear.

"I am the way, the truth, and the life: no man cometh unto the Father, but by me." — John 14:6

Entrance into heaven comes through:
- Repentance
- Faith in Jesus Christ
- Receiving Him as Lord and Saviour

Salvation is not earned by good works.

"For by grace are ye saved through faith." — Ephesians 2:8

¿What is Hell?

Hell is a real place of eternal separation from God.

"These shall go away into everlasting punishment." — Matthew 25:46

The Bible teaches:
- Hell was not created for humanity
- God desires all to be saved
- Separation from God is the result of rejecting Christ

"The Lord... is not willing that any should perish." — 2 Peter 3:9

¿Why Does God Allow Choice?

God created humans with free will.

"I have set before you life and death... therefore choose life." — Deuteronomy 30:19

Love requires choice. God does not force salvation.

¿Can I Be Sure of My Eternal Destiny?

Yes. The Bible teaches assurance of salvation.

"These things have I written unto you that believe... that ye may know that ye have eternal life." — 1 John 5:13

Assurance comes from trusting Christ, not feelings.

Faith Meets Real Life

- **When You Feel Afraid:** God offers peace through salvation.
- **When You Face Loss:** Heaven brings hope.
- **When You Make Choices:** Eternal perspective brings wisdom.
- **When You Share Your Faith:** You are offering eternal hope.

Pastoral Warning

Eternity is too important to ignore or postpone.

"Behold, now is the accepted time." — 2 Corinthians 6:2

Tomorrow is not promised.

A Clear Invitation

If you have never made a personal decision to follow Jesus Christ, today can be your day of salvation.

"Behold, I stand at the door, and knock: if any man hear my voice, and open the door, I will come in to him, and will sup with him, and he with me." — Revelation 3:20

Prayer of Salvation

Lord Jesus, I acknowledge that I am a sinner and that I need Your forgiveness. I believe that You died for my sins and rose again on the third day. Today I receive You as my Lord and Saviour. Forgive me, change me, and write my name in the Book of Life. I choose eternal life with You. Amen.

Discussion Questions

1. ¿What does the Bible teach about eternity?
2. ¿Why is heaven real?
3. ¿What determines where a person spends eternity?
4. ¿Why does God allow choice?
5. ¿How should eternal truth affect daily decisions?

Action Step (This Week)

- Reflect on your personal decision for Christ.
- Pray for someone who does not yet know Jesus.
- Live this week with eternal perspective.

Memory Verse

"I have set before you life and death... therefore choose life." — Deuteronomy 30:19

PERSONAL NOTES & ASSIGNMENT REFLECTION
Chapter 15
Personal Notes

Use this space to write your thoughts, questions, key ideas, Scripture verses, insights, or practical applications from this chapter. Reflect on how the truths you are learning apply to your daily life, decisions, and relationships.

"Thy word is a lamp unto my feet, and a light unto my path." *(Psalm 119:105)*

Assignment Reflection (if applicable)

____
____
____
____
____
____
____
____
____
____
____
____
____
____
____
____
____
____
____
____
____
____
____
____
____
____
____
____
____
____

Date: _______________________________

Signature / Initials: _______________________________

CONCLUSION

A LIFE EQUIPPED TO FOLLOW CHRIST

You have reached the end of *Equipped to Disciple Teens*, but this is not the end of your journey—it is a **new beginning**.

Discipleship is not a program to complete or a book to finish. Discipleship is a **lifestyle**—a daily decision to follow Jesus, learn from Him, and live out His truth with courage, humility, and love.

Throughout these chapters, you have explored foundational truths of the Christian faith:

- Your identity and purpose in Christ
- Salvation through Jesus alone
- Obedience through baptism
- The authority and power of God's Word
- Life in community with other believers
- Prayer, worship, and praise as daily practices
- Stewardship and godly character
- The fruit and gifts of the Holy Spirit
- Evangelism and sharing your faith
- The eternal reality of heaven and hell

Each of these truths is meant to shape **how you think, how you choose, and how you live**.

FROM KNOWLEDGE TO PRACTICE

True discipleship happens when truth moves from the page into real life.

"But be ye doers of the word, and not hearers only." (James 1:22)

You are now called to:

- Live out what you have learned
- Practice spiritual disciplines consistently
- Walk in obedience even when it is difficult
- Serve others with humility
- Share your faith with love and wisdom

Growth takes time. You will make mistakes. You will face challenges. But God is faithful, and He continues His work in you. "He which hath begun a good work in you will perform it until the day of Jesus Christ." (Philippians 1:6)

YOU ARE NOT ALONE

God never intended for discipleship to be lived in isolation. Stay connected to:
- Your local church
- Godly leaders and mentors
- Fellow believers who encourage you

Seek guidance. Ask questions. Keep growing.

"Iron sharpeneth iron; so a man sharpeneth the countenance of his friend." (Proverbs 27:17)

A CALL TO COMMITMENT

Today, you are invited to make a fresh commitment:
- To follow Jesus wholeheartedly
- To live according to God's Word
- To walk in holiness and love
- To be a light in your generation

Your age does not limit God's purpose for your life.

"Let no man despise thy youth; but be thou an example of the believers." (1 Timothy 4:12)

God desires to use you—right now.

FINAL BLESSING

May the Lord bless you and keep you. May He guide your steps and guard your heart. May His Word be a lamp unto your feet and a light unto your path. May you grow in wisdom, faith, and love. May the Holy Spirit strengthen you to live boldly for Christ in every season of life. May your life reflect the character of Jesus, and may you be equipped to disciple others just as you have been discipled.

The LORD bless thee, and keep thee: The LORD make his face shine upon thee, and be gracious unto thee: The LORD lift up his countenance upon thee, and give thee peace."

— Numbers 6:24–26

Go forward with confidence.
Live with purpose.
Walk with God.
To God be all the glory.

THEOLOGICAL GLOSSARY

Key Christian Terms Explained for Teens: This glossary explains important Christian words and ideas used throughout *Equipped to Disciple Teens*. Each definition is written clearly and simply to help students understand biblical truth and apply it to daily life.

Abiding in Christ: Living in close relationship with Jesus through faith, obedience, prayer, and trust. Abiding means depending on Christ daily for strength and guidance. (John 15:4–5)

Authority (Spiritual): Responsibility given by God to leaders to guide, protect, and teach His people according to Scripture, not to control or manipulate. (Hebrews 13:17)

Baptism: A public act of obedience in which a believer is immersed in water to show identification with the death, burial, and resurrection of Jesus Christ. Baptism does not save, but it shows faith. (Romans 6:4)

Bible (Word of God): The inspired Word of God that teaches truth, reveals God's will, and guides Christian faith and conduct. (2 Timothy 3:16)

Calling: God's purpose and direction for a believer's life, including how they serve Him and others. God calls people of all ages. (Jeremiah 29:11)

Church: The body of believers who follow Jesus Christ. The church is not a building, but a spiritual family where believers grow together. (1 Corinthians 12:27)

Conversion: The moment a person repents of sin and places faith in Jesus Christ, beginning a new life in Him. (2 Corinthians 5:17)

Discipleship: The lifelong process of learning from Jesus, obeying His teachings, and becoming more like Him. (Matthew 28:19–20)

Evangelism: Sharing the good news of Jesus Christ through words, actions, and lifestyle so others may know Him. (Mark 16:15)

Faith: Trusting God and believing His Word, even when we cannot see the outcome. True faith leads to obedience. (Hebrews 11:1)

Fruit of the Holy Spirit: The character of Christ produced in a believer's life by the Holy Spirit, including love, joy, peace, patience, kindness, goodness, faithfulness, meekness, and self-control. (Galatians 5:22–23)

Gospel: The good news that Jesus Christ died for our sins, rose again, and offers forgiveness and eternal life to all who believe. (1 Corinthians 15:3–4)

Grace: God's unearned favor toward humanity, through which we receive salvation and forgiveness—not by works, but by faith. (Ephesians 2:8–9)

Heaven: The eternal dwelling place of God, prepared for those who believe in Jesus Christ. Heaven is a place of peace, joy, and God's presence. (John 14:2)

Hell: A real place of eternal separation from God for those who reject Jesus Christ. God desires that all be saved. (Matthew 25:46; 2 Peter 3:9)

Holy Spirit: The third Person of the Trinity who lives in believers, convicts of sin, guides into truth, empowers service, and transforms character. (John 14:26)

Justification: God's act of declaring a sinner righteous through faith in Jesus Christ. (Romans 5:1)

Obedience: Choosing to follow God's Word and instructions out of love and trust. Obedience is evidence of genuine faith. (John 14:15)

Praise: Joyful expression of gratitude and celebration for what God has done. Praise declares God's goodness. (Psalm 34:1)

Prayer: Communication with God that includes talking, listening, worship, confession, and thanksgiving. Prayer builds relationship with God. (Jeremiah 33:3)

Repentance: A sincere turning away from sin and turning toward God, involving a change of heart and direction. (Acts 3:19)

Salvation: God's gift of forgiveness and eternal life received by faith in Jesus Christ. (Romans 10:9–10)

Sanctification: The ongoing process by which believers grow in holiness and become more like Christ. (1 Thessalonians 4:3)

Servant: A follower of Jesus who lives to serve God and others with humility and love. (Mark 10:45)

Spiritual Gifts: Special abilities given by the Holy Spirit to believers to serve others and build up the church. (1 Corinthians 12:7)

Stewardship: Faithfully managing the time, talents, and resources God has entrusted to us. (1 Corinthians 4:2)

Trinity: The biblical truth that God is one in essence and three in persons: Father, Son, and Holy Spirit. (Matthew 28:19)

Worship: Honoring God with our lives, obedience, and devotion—not only through music, but through daily living. (Romans 12:1)

BIBLIOGRAPHY

Scripture, Theology, and Discipleship Resources

This bibliography lists key Scripture sources and theological works that support the biblical teachings, doctrinal foundations, and discipleship principles presented in *Equipped to Disciple Teens*. The resources are suitable for pastors, teachers, youth leaders, and students seeking deeper study.

HOLY SCRIPTURE

The Holy Bible, King James Version (KJV). Public domain. Used throughout this work for all Scripture quotations unless otherwise noted.

DISCIPLESHIP & CHRISTIAN FORMATION

Bonhoeffer, Dietrich. *The Cost of Discipleship*. New York: Touchstone, 1995.
Coleman, Robert E. *The Master Plan of Evangelism*. Grand Rapids, MI: Revell, 2010.
Foster, Richard J. *Celebration of Discipline: The Path to Spiritual Growth*. San Francisco: HarperOne, 2018.
Hull, Bill. *The Complete Book of Discipleship: On Being and Making Followers of Christ*. Colorado Springs, CO: NavPress, 2006.
Ogden, Greg. *Transforming Discipleship: Making Disciples a Few at a Time*. Downers Grove, IL: InterVarsity Press, 2016.

THEOLOGY & DOCTRINAL FOUNDATIONS

Grudem, Wayne. *Systematic Theology: An Introduction to Biblical Doctrine*. Grand Rapids, MI: Zondervan, 1994.
Erickson, Millard J. *Christian Theology*. Grand Rapids, MI: Baker Academic, 2013.

Packer, J. I. *Knowing God*. Downers Grove, IL: InterVarsity Press, 1993.
Tozer, A. W. *The Knowledge of the Holy*. New York: HarperOne, 2009.

HOLY SPIRIT, SPIRITUAL GIFTS & CHRISTIAN LIFE

Fee, Gordon D. *God's Empowering Presence: The Holy Spirit in the Letters of Paul*. Peabody, MA: Hendrickson, 1994.
Stott, John R. W. *The Baptism and Fullness of the Holy Spirit*. Downers Grove, IL: InterVarsity Press, 1975.
Wimber, John. *Power Evangelism*. San Francisco: Harper & Row, 1992.

YOUTH MINISTRY & FAITH DEVELOPMENT

Dean, Kenda Creasy. *Almost Christian: What the Faith of Our Teenagers Is Telling the American Church*. Oxford: Oxford University Press, 2010.
Fields, Doug. *Purpose-Driven Youth Ministry*. Grand Rapids, MI: Zondervan, 1998.
Root, Andrew. *Revisiting Relational Youth Ministry*. Downers Grove, IL: InterVarsity Press, 2007.

EVANGELISM & MISSION

Stiles, Mack. *Evangelism: How the Whole Church Speaks of Jesus*. Wheaton, IL: Crossway, 2014.
Piper, John. *Let the Nations Be Glad! The Supremacy of God in Missions*. Grand Rapids, MI: Baker Academic, 2010.

CHRISTIAN CHARACTER & SPIRITUAL GROWTH

Willard, Dallas. *The Spirit of the Disciplines*. New York: HarperOne, 1998.
Manning, Brennan. *The Ragamuffin Gospel*. Colorado Springs, CO: Multnomah, 2005.

AUTHOR'S WORKS (DISCIPLESHIP SERIES)

Archbold, Frank S. *Equipped to Disciple: A Complete Guide for Christian Growth*. F. S. Archbold Publishing LLC, 2006, revised and expanded editions 2017, 2025.
Archbold, Frank S. *Equipped to Disciple Teens (Ages 13–15): Strengthening Faith, Identity, and Daily Christian Living*. F. S. Archbold Publishing LLC, 2025.

This bibliography is provided to encourage further study and deeper engagement with Scripture, Christian doctrine, and faithful discipleship for personal growth and ministry application.

CERTIFICATE OF COMPLETION

Note:

Use your mobile device to scan this QR code, which will redirect you to the template document for printing the certificate of completion of discipleship.